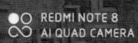

Kracow in Winter

A faint whisp of winter buffets
Snow that leads to the platform
Before the horror that was Plazow

At 4 Lipowa, however, optimism
And hope prevail as the winter
Snow glimpses the shiney enamelware
Hand machined; now symbolic of lives saved

Aboard the number 7, Poles
In mittens and individual caps and hats
Trundle into the still thickly walled Kazemeir
Where distant Klezmier music permeates the air

Rynek Glowny and St Mary's Basilica
Epitomise the true spirit of the place
Here is philosophy balanced
On the edge of an abyss

Retreating into distant centuries
Camelot warms the traveller with Intrigue and cherry vodka.
Tales of dragons and sulphur-
Stuffed sheep call out from the
Ramparts of Wawel that overlooks
Kracow in winter.

A distance from Otrakovice

Just now a gentleman in small
White boots pulling a trolley
Stopped
The trolley carried charcoal
And I took a small piece
It's crushed at the end of a Journal
Not preserved but there in
Smaller pieces
A distance now rom Otrakovice
Sharing thoughts with
Ludvik and Klara

Sharing a moment
Witnessed only by birds

Ancientness

It's not a recording
It's not a cockerel calling
Or equivalent
Drink or food

It's in your sandals
Which become your feet
And in between toes
Manipulating sand

It's all the ancient books
That fill libraries
From Oxford to Krakow
From Sophia to Alexandria

It's books, its books and
Wooden boats
That help you float
On a tide of
The present
However difficult that might be

Never arriving
Not ever discontent
Ever present
Never alone
Truly attracted to
Each and
Everything
Ancientness

Africa inspires

Positive energy can heal
The Universe
The Universe is <u>the</u>
Positive healer
Dreaming of Africa

I dreamt of
Running
The circumference
Of Lake Victoria

Bistro 16 (Sofia)

As the thunder roars
And the raindrops plunge
We are connected
Connected and protected
In Bistro 16

Scorchio Sofia

Just now a white
Umbrella flashed by
In Vitoshka street
It never saw me
But I saw it

Green trams

So beyond this stop
Where is this stop?
The next stop
To where?
Destination unknown
Might be a green
Tram arriving
Russian perhaps?
It may not be Bulgarian
But it's a proud green
Very green in fact
Painted or sprayed
With a smile
Waiting to be
Released on to
The lines
No choice
If you are a tram

Serendipity in the White City

The sweet smell of strawberries indoors
In May.
Tempt the wanderer to taste as
The rain patters
On frequently replaced
Market glass
You'll need to eat with friends not one or
two, but an
Afternoon to eat a kilo in good company

Maybe take them along to 'Samo Pivo'
And with bottles of labelled 'Red' read
Edgar Allen Poe celebrated on the bar wall
There watch 'The Raven'

Overlooking Lynx Island from the
Upper window of Kogo watch
Nature unfold perched at the confluence of
Two great rivers
Where even river rubbish
Enjoys their chance greetings
Past Robin Williams sprayed portrait ; grave smile,
To daylight spotlights on a foresaken river side, wooden clad warehouse ;
One can still glimpse the strawberry market at the top of the
Cobbled hill ,
Where people sell their clothes and their objects on
Their cobbled street.

'A bar has a longer history than its culture ' once said
And sat alongside Boban and friends we are all
Transported to ' Nova Varos'
One of a kind reflecting on more history than can
Possibly be consumed.

Craving attention with a room with a view , stories and music exchange
From 'Eleven Minutes' to 'Morphine ' and ' Cure for Pain '
Too later 'Turbo- Folk' - provocative and raunchy as the city often can be

' Cash or card?' ' Korak by Korak ' let the White City wash over the walker
In a maze of streets where it's fun to get lost.
Step by step , unhurried , with no joy in
Agitating over it.

Yesterday is old news but a long time ago
Is nonetheless essential
The past is all about roots and heroes and chance meetings with beauty;
From Ana Bajovic set to

Mapacha

Mapacha is a coffee shop
In Paje
Tended lovingly and named so
After the owners twins
Where today
Karmen nurses a swollen
Puss-ridden leg raised on a stool
Wishing for the hand of Christ to heal it
Miglane ever philosophical. Ever hopeful
Always loving
Flowers dance in a wooden boat
And a vacant space opposite
Awaits the opening of a
Business venture to energise
Weary travellers and locals alike
Relaxing to the slow beat of Mapacha

Sleepy Sibenick

There are playful starlings in sleepy Sibenick
They appear as the golden sun
Hangs momentarily then wraps its
Glow along the nearby coastline

There are fishing boats in sleepy Sibenick
Many of them; some old and wooden with
A fisher buoy
Who fishes all day
And the Jadroliniza passenger vessels
Deposit locals and travellers alike in
Vodice
That proudly remembers its war dead

There are bottles of Babbich in
Sleepy Sibenick
Many from the many vines
That hug the mountain sides
For miles and miles

There are lovely people in sleepy Sibenick
A pink house on 3 floors
Built on the garden of his
Mother's house

There are fresh tomatoes in
Sleepy Sibenick
Picked by the kind hand of
Ivo's wife who
Never does anyone a bad turn
Only good
There is much more to sleepy Sibenick

The Legend Bar

Perched in the far corner
Or on Thursday by the sink
There you might find Neno
The mate of young Patrick!

Waxing lyrical from
Dali to heroine
To not appreciate such intellect
Would be a sin

A kidnapped son
And a cherry shot
A young man's father
Forgotten not in Zagreb

Pottering in Oasis

Mop the floor with a mop
But no squeezy bucket
Check the ice machine
Have a swim
Log on

Cup of grand Yorkshire tea
Wipe a surface
Wander rooms
With ipod on shuffle
Another swim
Log on

Up-date journal
Read a little
Contemplate poem ideas

Guitar practice
Log on

Darkness at 5 in September
The day has pottered by
Pottering
Pottering in Oasis

16 Lions

From 'Tame Impala(s)
To 'the Cat Empire'
A possible soundtrack
For both teaming impala
And elusive cats

Tanzanian skies are huge
Shifting effortlessly
Funnelling the evening
Sunshine
Glistering dawn grass
Enjoyed by elephants

Aboard Gilberts
Much repaired 'rickety steed'
Infinite travellers
Exchange such smiles of good fortune
And stories
Dreams
Just 2 years away
Already begun

A hand painted wooden doll
Always cherished
Forever a reminder
Of sixteen lions

Michamvi

A pillow carefully placed
A rickety wooden pier
Dancing latino in the sand;barefoot
Time standing still
Exchanging stories

Wishing
The electricity would
Fail for longer
Connections and love
Miriam briefly from Michamvi

A brief return to England

Warwick services
A Zombieland
Of stooped masked
Conditioned
Un-thinking
Accepting
Victims of media lies
Cards only for food
Get me out of England

AGIBA

The azure of such a sea is timeless
The land now above once below
How many years has that taken
Who cares
But what lies above
And below

Seashells hold a clue
Still presiding
Below turquoise waters
For they hold the secrets
Of time
That are meant to be
Remained unlocked

In the 'WALLED-OFF'

I'm glad I stuck around
And was patient
Im glad you didn't ditch me
Watching a 'munchkin' do handstands
Against an artists painted fireplace

As the gentle Easter light of Bethlehem
Illuminates the wall
Shadowing the tension filled labyrinths
Of the Old City
Jerusalem

CAIRO

Il Pennello

Aged bark flanks
A canyon wall
Supporting American Diners
And false Ivy

A china cat
Empty of money
And fake paint
Appearing dry

Flanked by manicured bush
And flashes of purple
Road 9 presents
Itself more peacefully on Fridays

'Happy Halloween' replaced by
Neon Heinekein
As November ends
An hexagonal glass prism
Proudly displays snow men
Pepper pots and Santa hats
All for sale

Petit cuboidspeakers
Often dress an
Abdomen high table
Positioned for friends

From Morrissey to James with James
Leonard Cohen to Duran Duran
The Sakara unit always gold
But the banter usually priceless

Eyes left a neon-blue Mercedes
And a forever dirty windscreen
Graffited by a child's finger
That only infrequent rain
Might possibly erase

Ashraf sometimes sports a
Beige gentleman's jacket
But mostly suited and
Always a gentleman

He'll greet you, if you wish
With a wine and a smile

Or more usually a smile
And a wine or whatever you wish
In Il Pennello
A favourite place of mine

Ohrid Lake

"Hello, can I share your
Sandwich please?"

Ezra spreads the hard butter
With her index finger confidently
And singing a made up tune
to

"I love to spread this butter
I spread it all the time"

"Do you need help Ezra?"

"Let me try to do it?"

Ezra (still humming)

"I spread it all time"

"Mr Michael why do you wear glasses?"

"Are you old?"

"No Ezra. Well maybe I am.
Young people wear glasses too"
Even around Ohrid Lake
Macedonia

Chilled Azher

Below a stone balcony
And beyond an artificial lake
The citadel glows
In the freezing January air
Illuminating newly weds

Two strangers meet
For the first time
Circulating a famous
Park gradually
Emptying its guests

Two remain
Connecting, smiling, connected
And a day later
Almost making love
But more intimate and
Closer than even that

Brief moments of tenderness
In an often cruel
And melancholy world

Maadi Morning

A ghostly linen net tries and falls
Fuelled by and whispered upon by a
Cool Maadi breeze
A sudden waft creates
Movement and dance

Symbolic of possible chance
Encounters again
Birds chirp happily all around
A distant dog bark 'peters' out
As the great green canopies
Summon energy windwards
And skywards
Ona Maadi morning

A Maadi Tree

'Hey tonight
I saw a tree again
And in the depths of you
I felt your roots again'

Balconies

On a random balcony
It's good to use your time productively
Tonight I'm adjacent
To a huge palm tree
Swaying provocatively
In a Cairean weekend wind
Looking forward to
Another night
As the corona fear continues to bite
All but the most
Discerning of thinkers

Self- Isolation

So, 'holed-up' in Cairo
Glass of wine in hand
All that I know is
The media should be banned

Propaganda abounds calculated fear
Taking us down a garden path
Where everyone must steer

I prefer free thinking
The 'ruse' behind the scenes

So I'll carry on drinking
And eating baked beans

Whatever is happening
We may never know the truth
And whatever the future may bring us
All will be fine, 'God strewth'

Corona is a virus just that
A lingering one of conspiracy

Full of lies so fat
Few can clearly see

When whatever is coming comes
And gazing up at the moon
I'm sure a brighter future looms
(I hope)

A Mayor's House

Did you feel this coming?
A storm over The Nile
Rubbish tossed skywards
Landing by its ancient banks

Did you feel this coming?
Falling out of love
And wondering whether you ever in it?
Searching for love

Did you see this coming?
A random walk in Giza
An ordinary balcony
Overlooking the extraordinary

Did you feel this coming?
A life less ordinary
Appreciated by few
Captured in a diary

Did you feel this coming?
A time of fear
Where all your instincts
Point elsewhere
Did you feel this coming?

Somewhere to go at 3am

Jag :'Fuzzy' today
And if I see you at 3am
It will be to dwell
On the gifts of the present
A life lived
And how to cook 'spinach'

Next to Never
Petering the Nile at a necessary pace
Birds that were
Always there
Sang as if in the
'Albert Hall'
Alleluyah

So onwards I go
Oh so very distanced
Fridge full
With the promise of
Freshness

Promised in an
Uncertain world
Where 'my' trees
Have all the company they need
Even though I'm momentarily gone

A whisper of a
Lockdown in Cairo
No problem!
We the resilient
Have been here before

Mrs Lockhart's 'Nile Garden'

A farm labourer's cottage in Redhills
Complete with the 'Good Life'
Greenhouse and fiery red bantam

Chickens running free
A coal bunker to trap and intrigue
Adventurous siblings
A rickety, rusty swing
That helped set daily
World record leaps
Recorded by a twig
A long narrow lawn
Where gymnastic super-hero
Uncles, would mesmerise with
Walking on their hands
And 'flic-flacs!'

Adjoining number 2 Redhills
Is a very different garden
The lovingly tended earth
Of Mrs Lockhart and
Bearded Scottish Eddie
Sacred strawberries luscious

Beneath a 'then expensive'
Green net; a Sunday treat
For Michael, Julie and Carol
The grateful siblings next door
Red Admirals and many other
Breeds of butterfies
Delighting in the array of colours
That stopped many a walker
And casual driver
To simply stop, look and smell

Weekend deliveries of 'Beano'
And 'Dandy' from the back of a Peugeot estate
Newspapers for the grown-ups
And mo-jo's and black jacks
For us all!

Beyond the garden and
Its precarious wall
Baring left
A different garden
By the 'Limes Hotel'
Still going now and
Still teaming with daffodils
That these days appear much earlier
Picking rose-hips and blackberries
From free road side bushes

Comment [UT]:

Later turned into beautiful
Jam, carefully labelled in a
Larder on Fell Lane
Grandma Taylor's larder
At the base of the next hill
In the road
A stream ran under it and
Still does to a haunted
House on the hill and a tip
A tip where 'flic-flac'
Uncles helped siblings
Make go-karts' affectionately
Named 'bogies', firm discarded
Pram wheels, bits of wood
And orange bailing twine
From the farm to help us
Steer at 100mph down the
Perilous 'Slapestones Hill'

A quarry beyond for
Climbing down into
And collecting empty golden shells
From a secret firing range

Follow the river below
Teaming with brown trout
Along fields segregated in
The summer by electric fences
Tested by children with blades of grass
Along the river to a place of
Intense adventure and natural beauty
Snow-drops and primrose
Wild rhubarb and thistles
Rope swings from the tallest branches
Fixed by fearless folk from 'Townhead'
A narrow river bank trail
Paved 'Black – Rock' where
Even the strongest swimmer
Might be sucked into the whirlpools
Below, then onwards to a
Favourite stopping point for
All Penrithians
Pokey Dubs!!

Penrithians who walked there
With lemon curd sandwiches
And ribena in plastic bottles

A viaduct with a green ladder
That only the bravest would climb
To a railway line where new electric trams
FiZZED past
Lighting fires with matches and
'Acquired farm paraffin'
Knocking down the biggest conkers
With stones and sticks-
All day sometimes
Only a short walk then
Across a few small fields
To the clunking milking parlour
The smell of a sileage pit
Greeting a lone bull
The orchard of Sally and Tommy Colson
And then back down the hill
To Mrs Lockhart's garden
To a simpler life
Where imagination and nature
Made every season magical

Back in 'Lockdown Cairo'
Like the rest of the world
One day is merging into another
As it did as a child in Redhills

Today I followed an under-pass,
Socially distanced of course
Past heaps of rotting rubbish
A lady sat completely in black
With both hands held skywards
Sat amongst the filth
Random puppies and scraggly cats
Lost chickens and geese
The under-pass then narrowed
Slowly, to reveal
The Nile. The Nile!

Between its swaying reeds
The sun glistened on its
Ripples and garden banks
The banks of Ancient Memphis
Where the Holy family
Possibly once boarded
A sailing boat which carried
Them towards scorching
Southern Egypt

To Nile gardens full of
Green and 'without limits' indeed
As limitless as love and
Without the conditions of
An endless summer and always fresh

Feeling safe in nature
I sat awhile and
Thought of Mrs Lockhart's garden
Ancientness
 Hankering after a simpler life to which
We may all soon return

Kanal Street Tree

Tonight I watched you
And in the roots of you
I felt the depth of you

Balancing Bread

Today a
Taxi driver
Asked me
What I thought
About Sisi
As we passed through
Sadat Square
As we did so
A circus cyclist swept past
With bread on his head
Weaving In and out of the traffic on a bike in
Sadat Square
Balancing on the edge of
Survival to feed his family

Maadi Mornings

Satellite dishes seem
Rested on a Maddi morning
A universal pause button
Pressed momentarily
To allow a glimmer
Of nature back in

A snap shot of
A once Ancient City
Ready to be reclaimed
Now more than ever

Estoril

I think is a place
In Spain
But tonight
It's a gem of a place
Below 'The Lotus Bar'
And across from
'The Café RIche'
Where I met
Kashef

Who took me home
Bought me a beer
And introduced me
To the joy of diving

Vermilion Street

Laura roams Vermilion Street
Today I called her
But my neighbour
Called her 'Baby'

Her tummy and lisks
Are mottled like a cow
Basking today in dust-free sunshine
Waiting for vermilion

When it comes
It will be mercury red
It's perfume
Wafting down our
Street
Igniting it.

Today the roads and streets
Are presenting themselves differently
More bird song-so much more!

The clunking of an old bike
Yielded a 'Good morning Sir'
'Good morning' I replied
I called for Baby
Who skipped up road 86
To greet me
And a delivery man
For whom I left
The door ajar
Was so grateful
As I am today
Just to be alive.

EGYPT

Flanking a Lagoon

There are showgirls legs on
The Sinai mountains as the
Sun disappears in a Red Sea glow

Lower down the mountain
At the base in fact are
Off the shelf dark glasses
Fossilised in Christ

3am Pit Fires

Fire lights and frames
Distant Saudi mountains
A freshly placed
Gnarled log
Burning because
It has no other option
Than to do so

This is the day after
Yesterday only
Three hours ago
As the sun rises and the
Fire now glows
The Red Sea shimmers

Today I will learn to
Windsurf upon it

Habu Temple (Oh Faye)

Oh 'Faye' with the silence
Of a new water colour
Close to ever present bird sone
And razor edge granite underfoot
A fallen Pharaoh lies peacefully
An artist dressed in black
Away from the blazing heat
Almost alone in the midday shade
Enveloped in mystery and pain

'Pearl of the South'

The Pearl of the South
Has an arched entrance
And a dream catcher
Fluttering in a Dahab sky
Dancing to the distant
Dulcit tones of
Violins
A painter's wooden table
Painted white
And laden with fresh strawberries
Skilfully and lovingly
Bringing life to Abrahim
And momentarily
A faceless lady
Adorned in aqua green
Kneeling and passive
Awaiting tea

Happenchance today
In Hasan's courtyard
Strewn with yellow cushions
Random themed tyres and
Hexagonal turquoise cobblestones

Hasan, hands on head
Watches Abrahim emerge
Between a mature pine

And a favourite bush
Smiling now at beautiful
'Yuli' in February sunshine

Oh Faye (Part II)

Oh Faye with the silence of a
Watercolour
Close to ever present bird song
And razor edged granite under foot
A fallen Pharaoh lies peacefully
Amongst white pink Habu sandstone
Supporting an artist
Dressed in black
Almost alone in the midday shade
Enshrined in mystery

The Golden Dog of the Lagoona

Dogs are naked
All the time!
In Dahab they
Are naked, free and happy
In their by the Red Sea
Mainly in shade during the day
Chasing headlights
And cyclists
By night
Golden is a girl
Spending time
Being temporarily adopted
Like a 'holiday let'
Without a kennel
Her brother is different
(Apart from the obvious!!)
They share the same
Deep brown hazelnut eyes
Flanked by jet black
Eye lashes and markings
They don't bark
At certain bicycles
Parked up at the Lagona
Room 21

Sinai Heals

Sandwiched between
The Red Sea and
The Sinai mountains
Lies a peaceful, invisible
Filling

A path snakes both
North and South
Sometimes claiming
The face of late nights
Cyclists
Faces here heal
Younger than before
Much younger and
Rapidly
Cleaner, smoother; as new!

A broken heart
Denied access to a mother's funeral
Separations and divorces
Betrayals and abuse

All gently healed
At a pace as timeless
And as ancient
As a hand line
Tossed out by a fisherwoman
From the past at dawn,
On the shore of Abu Galum

In Ramsey and Paulo's
Jazz dances
On a calm night sea
The peace and healing of
Sinai that takes good
Care of us all

A timeless energy
That only becomes stronger
With time

Sinai truly heals ......

The Jet Black Dog of Dahab

The Jet Black Dog of Dahab
Is the size of a wolf
With the eyes of Christ

He may follow you
Home after midnight
Even follow you on
For salami and fresh milk
And nestled by your feet
Fleeting flashes of white hair
Glisten in
The moonlight
The Black Dog of Dahab
Content and asleep

He will be gone
When you wake
Asleep by the shore
Of the Red Sea
Oblivious to a meditator
Who shares the space

Seeing in the dawn
Where the sea
Rolls differently in
In Dahab
Though it has no choice
The Sea
Seems to roll its voice
Turning into dogs
Slumbering on its shore
Along with a half-naked
Man, covered in shingle

Pyramid Builders

Amidst a stormy moon
Such as this
Who needs nails
When there is granite!

Lovers by an early morning Sea

What floats on your mind
As you watch a calm sea
Or is laundried around in a storm?

The motion of the sea and the sound
Is the motion of the sea and its sound
Relentless in just being
No wave the same

The boundaries too it
Are all too often man-made
Only in the spaces inbetween
Does it 'nip away' unobtrusively
Through time

Its sound is a 'universal symphony'
With no practice required
As timeless and as short
As the universe we currently know

You See?

What you 'sea' is
What you get with the sea!
Never forces anything
Going with its flow and ending up
Where it ought

The approach to Dahab

There are elephant feet
Planted in the desert
En route to Dahab
Their toes are carefully
Manicured in sand

'Petit Pylons'

Random bin bags
And
Pylons

Aligned as small people
Disappearing into
The Ocean

Happy Cars

There's a silver beetle
With punctured tyres'
Below me
Always parked up
Restore me!
But not too much

Trundling around Dahab
At all hours
Are Isuzu's
With Bedouins
Hanging out of the
Window
Watching, staring
On mobiles to the mafia
Toothless Youssef has a
White cab
 To get out you
Have to lift the
Passenger door
Even if you don't need a lift
You hop in anyway
Into Youssefs happy car

In Cairo after a while
Mostly you stop hearing
The unnecessary beeps and
Beeps and beeps
But in Dahab it's impossible
The Isuzu's are
Sinister carriages
That don't belong in
The magic land of Sinai
I prefer to take a
Bike with a basket –
Preferably a yellow one

Sinai

Let me be a rainbow rising
Want to be your
Love light from above
Shine on Sinai

Saleem Says

I met an aged man
That looked like
Omar Sharief
In the street

He was sat with a beautiful
Girl whore
Arms were ablaze
With tattoos'

We talked off Sinai
And where we had
All had come from

Zohra's House-Tunis

At dusk a sturdy tractor
Approached steadily
Up a dusty Tunis track
Passed the home of
Zohra the ultra legend
And Rodenbeck
Who brought the history
Of Cairo to life

The tractor slowly trundled
By passed me
It was covered in bright
Lights
And from Belarus
Because it said so
It was clearly old
But disguised by lights
Presented shining new
Not as old however
As the petrified forest
Ran through today

Nor the pharaonic
Black rock
Used by the pharaohs
To build the great bases
Of the Giza pyramids
On that very stone
A wade Ibex yellow jeep
Also stopped where the
Tractor passed me by
And I was handed candles
From the driver for Zohra's
Surprise birthday cake
Not long afterwards we all
Danced and sang
In Zohra's house upon ancient land
Celebrating the spirit of
This metronomic runner
Zohra Merhabit

Tunis Village

Tonight we slept in
Fits and starts
To the rhythm of Tunis
In our hearts

Ana Fora

If depression rears
It's head in Cairo
Head straight for
Anafora

I was rude to
Dr Ahlam there
Three years ago
Now look where
That got me?
A friend for life

Out of Egypt

I'm dismayed to
Return to this damned
Country where you see
The sun in the sky
About as often
As a diamond in a
Camel's behind
Get me back to Esna
Back to Egypt!!

Windmills in the desert

A five land highway
Forges through Sinai's ancient
Mountains
The bases of windmills
Lipped by rubbish
And sloppy excavations
The turbines turn slowly
In a breathless wind
Labouring and pointless
In a wasteful 'pre-covid'
World
Inventions to supply
Human greed and waste
And paved by camels
And Bedouins
That knowingly
Still plod the desert
'Toy town' – El Gouna
Appears in the distance
Perfectly manicured
Sterile and unreal
Yet nonetheless peaceful
In Athena

Hathor 100km

No one knows
How the turquoise
From Sarabit
Was extracted
For the bracelets
And iconic death mask

Of the boy King

Two ultra runners
On the eve of the Hather 100
Speculate about
Walking this land before
In another time

Mohshen and Maria
Nicha and Zohra
Runners from all over
Egypt

Ran this ancient land
Champion Wadi Ibex
The Maadi Runners
And the utter joy
Freedom
Of running!!

Heavens Rubin

Today a lone ship
Glided through the night
Over a dead calm Red Sea
Illuminated by a full moon
Then moored itself over
A solitary sacred reef
Shimmering in early morning sunshine
Seemingly expectant
Of random bubblying caucasians
Intent on revealing
The hidden secrets of Daedalus

'Those were the days' rang out
Following the iconic timeless tunes of
Abel el Halim Hafik
Divers hopeful and expectant
Of further treasures

One such treasure found us
Curious and posing in the depths
Of the blue
The suns refracted rays
Made her glow like polished silver
As she shimmered past at eye level

A gathering of hanging bubbling Caucasians
And then dropped her hammerhead to one side
To smile and wink maybe

WOMEN

Nobody's Puppy

Perched neatly on a dimly lit step
Petit and lithe
In pensive mood
A Genevan beauty
Artificially lit
Beneath the summits of Sinai

Spanish guitar gently
Permeates connections and addictions
Passion and craving
Searching for meaning
With belly laughs

Countryside 'Green Miles'
Along meandering lands
Life lessons from grandparents
Serendipity

Tattoos' sex and alcoholism
Rock 'n' roll
Of lives lived on the edge
Violins and concentration camps

Running towards and not away
With and not against the flow
Beneath a Bedouin Milky Way
Or the silence of a Red Sea Bay

From Guadalupe to Bogota
Alabama Monroe to Chardonnay
Two kindred spirits
Less lost

A Time of Ancient Gifts

Ahead the great stretch
Of an illuminable desert
The winding flood of the Nile
Lapping the sand
The distant pyramids swimming
In the haze
Two lovers nestled
In sand
Wired to an ancient earth
Connected once more and as always
To this universe
Meeting again
Under the kind and knowing eye
Of a watchful sphinx

Aloft by the Pyramids
Let the energy roar from
Random red roses and
Smiles; oh those smiles galore

Re-united ancient travellers
Now stylised by a painter's hand
Lighted candles illuminating
Colonial teak balconies
Eyes fixed and sparkling
Left shoulders dropped
Hair and skin Egyptian golden
And in the morning still glowing

The scent of Gopal
On the banks of
The Euphrates
The gentle lilt
Of an Oud in Gurdjuef
The voice of an angel
Permeating today a more
Balanced universe
Re-connecting with nature
Simplicity in silent peace

There are fields on the edge of
Ramat Gan
And in the shadows of
Redhills too
Fields beyond this
Artificial world
And beyond all doubt and pain
Nature envelops the travellers
Picking paths from the heart
Random kisses
Rivers running within our
Souls and gently
Opening up those hearts
Day by day dreams turned
Into a 'Ministry of Love'

.... a single grain of sand
Caught on the great granite
Base of Giza witnessed only
By two ....

Irish Judy

Judy listens
I mean really listens ......

A metered stride
Along the Caironean Corniche
Whistling by
Random thoughts and
Buildings alike
The 'turn' is reached at an aqueduct
And oh what a turn!
Reflections in Santiago

Today saw unusual
January rain in Cairo
Making a hilly 'Rope-pull'
A welcome relief
A belated birthday celebration
And 'November Rain'
Ends the perfect morning
With guitars that cry

If Dina were here

What? Right now?
As I go to bed alone?
What if Dina were here
Where we've been before
A gentle spirit skirting
A Major's house
Stone walls
With grafitted 'Stable People'
Or Road 9
As the birds waken and a 'poet' stumbles
Down the street
Atomic
Coral injuries
Corresponding pain
Mutual affection and care
Whether that be in Sinai or Rhoda Island
Alexandria or Kigali
Road 86 or the Nilometer
Love is love
Connecting so powerfully
A last breath from Cohen

Zita – Hungary Eyes

Zita …………

With a smile and hungry hazelnut eyes
Driven to Adliyah
Savouring pumpkin soup
And replaying a possible future
Contemplating
Our encounter in the 'Grand Mosque'
A romantic encounter
That brought two travellers
Together
Momentarily in a fleeting dream

Mira

On a hot summer's day
In Sofia, I was robbed!
I made it to Jerusalem

But retreated from the noisey
Commercialised stations of the cross
To sit alone by the grave of
Oscar Schindler
Confused and dismayed

Stepping off a bus in
Bethlehem
It was there I met an angel
And bought her a peach
And I was shown Palestine
In all its glory
Her name is Mira
And we met on the street

The Heart of Torit

This morning in late May
The stalactite fretwork
Of the front terrace of
The Mena house
Is encased carefully
In scaffolding
Protecting the wooden
Craftsmanship
Inspired by a golden
Age of Islamic architecture

Olivia from south Sudan,
Absorbs appreciatively from her balcony
The splendour of the Mena gardens
And rues the grand palm tree
Obscuring the flattened tip of Kafu
Sharing tale of Irish
Grandfather John
And clever uncle Bill
Adopted as a son

To contend the challenges
Of growing up in the US
BLACK!
Olivia gazes into the eyes of
Ninety plus Irish Grandfather John
That capture the
Humility and compassion
So sadly lacking in the world today

Two philosophical strangers
One young, one young at heart
Glorious Egyptian May morning
Rapturous at first
Delighting in birdsong, music
Spontaneous dancing and singing
Until the conversation turns
To George Floyd from Minnesota
It is then that I picture
Then a derelict Mena house
Charred remains of the Islamic
Wooden architecture and fallen trees
The world is heading for such
An apocalyptic crossroads
And two philosophers
One crying now
Ponder how to transform it all
The positive energy that
Does exist in the world
Maybe bottle the essence of
Irish Grandfather John
Into a perfume and spread
It furtively from silent gliders
Throughout this world

The Pyramids still overlook
Knowing and listening

The Gem of Belgrade

Sweet smelling strawberries
Waft the steps surrounding
The indoor market
Luring the walker
To the river below
And there glistering
In its water
Lies a gem
A reflection of a lady
With the eyes of a child
And the smile of an angel
Today solitary
Not thinking but still
If fortunate to catch
A glimpse of this gem

Or better still
A brief encounter
You'll feel her love and care
Her selfless spirit
Go down to the river
Her name is Nada Popovic

Angel Amira

December 28th
An angel made
Her way to heaven
I never got to say
Goodbye but
Now in the sky
Amira's kindness
Shines and shines
Forever
On her husband
Her children
On EBIS Concordia and the ROYAL
And all of
Egypt actually

IN ZAIN
IN ZAIN
To be 'In -Zain 'is a
Glorious state of now .
The right here and now where
Time can stand still.

'In - Zain' you will find
Raw beauty , Intelligence and
Surreal tenderness.
Oh and the smile!
A smile negating the need for a passport!

'In Zane' you know love
That comes to you without warning.
You know your spirit;
You know your soul.
You know you are alive ,
You feel SO alive
'In Zain'

Insane to be 'In Zain?'
A perfect place to be........

NUBIAN GEM

Jet black hair, fresh smelling
Wafted by an Abu Simbel breeze......

Aged, rickety and beige the 84 sleeper ,
Jerks and shunts its way tentatively
Towards Aswan
On board two connected strangers
Encounter a silent meeting.
Nubian gems sparkle in the desert
Like the smile and energy of
Fawal captured over and over
As the beige buffet car trundles to
 final stop and a solo traveller smiles
Awardly too.

Love and light, oh so much light
Still pervade this transported temple
And today so much more
For in an ancient chamber
The smile of a Nubian gem
Lights up the centuries
And the soul of the same solo traveller .
Outside the sea is calm
And bares witness to a second 'chance ' encounter in as many days.
Connected once again through
The hidden language of natural signs and symbols

Jet black Algerian hair , fresh smelling still wafted by an Abu Simbel
breeze..........

RANDOM

Perspective

Leaning forward I felt my
Selfish hamstring pull and
Felt so lucky to even
Have one
Rubbishing about where to run
I could wake up in Syria
Toothless and traumatised

Rock Rockers

Flies
TE data
Intolerance
Muslims
Christians
Uber
Ali
Cheating
Egyptians
Abba Puppets
Chicken street strips
Flower man
More lies
Meltdown in Cairo

Love Is

A zip
A secretary
A moment in time
A random cigarette
A flirtation
Wonderful moments
Beautiful feelings
Ahh – no words

Ceiling Fan

An angled eye
With scalloped blades
Contemplates and lures
Dismemberment

Bedouin tea
Remnants
And Cape Bay

Sleep

Do birds sleep
And if so how and when?
Maadi trees
Sleep also
Still even in a wind sometimes

'Le petit – balconies'

Last night on a bunkered balcony
Set back from an alleged infected street
It was teaming with and life and friendship
And several bottles of wine!

Not to mention
Oranges and Leonard
Primal scream and onions
A playscript on life
Emerging
In these troubled times

Mr James

Mr James
Has a Sakara belly
Especially after the summer

Radiance

Radiance is everywhere!
Stones with seashells in them
The beginning of creation underfoot
A mesmeric landscape of wonderment
Where the conflict between

Global cultures
Should pause if not rest awhile
It's time to find happiness
In a world fully of calamity

How to live more

Live more
Live a dangerous life
Full of curiosity

Empty what is full
Fill what is empty
Live more

Haikus

Solo travellers
Eating usually alone
Finding atmosphere

Annie, Rob and Mike
Talk of markets at Christmas
No niggles today

Ancient Greece and grammar
Fuels an invincible run
Great start to the day

Oscar Wilde

Oscar Wilde once said
'Positive energy can heal the universe'
I said immediately
The universe is the positive healer

Blond Tickles and Life Pressure

Connecting with John Grant
Echoes of Elton John
In the sunshine dancing
With festival cider 'in cid-yer'
A chance meeting on a train
Leading to many connections
And ultimately great intimacy

Who'll take this pain way?
You me John
You sing 'there are children who have
Cancer
I can't compete with that indeed
Blond tickles and life pressure
I can't compete with that
I just can't compete with that

Intrigue and cherry vodka

Tales of dragons and sulphur-stuffed
Sheep call out from the
Ramparts of Warwel that overlooks
Krakow in winter

Irony

Love being at airports with music
On shuffle, especially when
'Show some respect' blasts out
At the boarding signal

Joker Indeed

If life was thirty cards
I'd have surely found a Joker by now
The card would find me
Self pity
In the form of a fatherly punch to the face

Tonight I crawled inside a fridge

Not exactly
Pull out all the trays
And the contents of a life
That wasn't mine anyway
Re-creating water into ice
A human form
Into a new life

The man in white

Greeted by
Man covered in white
Paint this morning

We drank orange juice
From a wine glass
It was good it
Wasn't boring
It was almost like
The blues

Omar sighs with the lyrics
And Carol emerges from
Her sleep
Cat like

One by One

One by one
A relationship begins
And ends almost
As quickly as it begins
Especially if you follow

What you ought too!
Ksenia is a Russian
That lives far from Moscow
Voluptuous
Which just isn't enough

Comfort is

Hot water bottles
Steamy bowls of water with
Vicks to help you breath
Beans on toast with HP sauce
Mulled wine on the ski slopes
Alone above a pinnacle
Surrounded by clown fish
The scent of a woman
You love
Strawberries straight from
The ground
Finding a new place
With a new friend randomly
'we are stable people'
The safety of a familiar bed
The smell
Of a new born baby's head
Knowing you are
Misfit
In this crazy crazy world

Spectre by Radiohead

On a sparkling cloud
When you're in the music
Zone
'The Bends'
Songs on shuffle
Often touch your soul

And on bended knee
'Demons' eventually arrives

Replenishing the Beverage

South from Aswan
Feluccas said
Tonight boarded by
Friends
Illuminated by a
Full moon
Friends replenish
Their beverages
Until

'I love you Bethany'
Your spirit
Is quite simply
Overwhelming
Marry Leo

I returned to Beverly
Hills, to building 59
Thinking of my friends
And happy I did so

LEO

Conversations with Leo
Begin with
'The National'
From Cincinnati Ohio
The rest is electric
Intoxifying infact!

Mirror Image

I'm looking at
The mirror image
Of a sister
I wished I had

In the tunnel of love

Meandering thro

Memories with friends
Thro' Edinburgh
And ending up in China

Fired on fuelled
On Egyptian electricity
(Wait or the end)

Proceeding into pickled
Beetroot
That smells and tastes
Exactly as beetroot should
I look at Suzanne's
Outer door
And think of Attaba
And the scalloped canopy
Of the Windsor hotel
In the tunnel of love

A narrative

A narrative on life
Is a narrative
It's certainly not a
Massacre
It's a narrative

Death

'Stop worrying!
No one gets out of
This life alive?

Common sense

Common sense and a
Sense of humour
Are the same thing

Moving at different speeds
A sense of humour
Is just
Common sense dancing

The Incident

Seven cats perished
In an inferno below me
The owner and his
Mother were
Brought a ladder
I wasn't there
Thankfully
But with no
Escape
I just had to leave
A building
That witnessed
Such a terrible incident
Two in fact

Haikus are shit

Haikus are just shit
Syllables are forced to fit
No space to show wit

Mona from The South

Makes terrible place mats
And today I bought
An even 'terriblier' box
Unseen but I love it!

Mr John 'Tufty' Roman

The goal remains
Further than the reach
Written but
Never sung by the writer
But released at a time

When those close to
Mr Roman reflect
On his untimely goodbye

'Roaming' the world
Seemingly alone
Marvelling curiously
At detail
Respecting, appreciating
And loving
The beauty of the world
And retreating into
Buddhist charts
Away from those
Living a duller life

MOBY

We're all rising
As the smoke settles
On addictions

BREAK UPS

Only in the
Agony of Parting
Do we look
Into the depths
Of love

CONVERSATIONS WITH TRUE FRIENDS

Conversations with true friends are unfailingly good
Even when they turn out bad

YEAST IN THE AIRING CUPBOARD

Yeast in the airing cupboard
Birds Trifle in the fridge
Farleys rusks in the larder
Vicks on a shelf

Mousetrap and Buckaroo under a bed
A Jack Russel pup in the outside loo

Star Trek at seven
Sherry in the sherry cabinet

A fathers parents at the door
Yelling abuse
Mothers clothes strewn on the lawn
Scared to pick them up

Yeast in the airing cupboard

F**R ! I LOST YOUR BROTHER**

On a February evening in Zamalek
I picked up two Baladi's
Barely alive, shivering under a car
Coated in oil

A baladis eyes see deep in to yours
And into the eyes of Hepshepshut
The sister of the brother
Is two years now but,
F****R, I lost your brother

NO SHECKELS

Catching a bus in Eilat
Without sheckels is okay
You'll get to where you are going
Anway!

Printed in Great Britain
by Amazon